CLUES TO AMERICAN GARDEN STYLES

Cover drawing:
   Dumbarton Oaks, Washington, D.C.

Let every house be placed, if the person pleases, in the middle of its plat as to the breadth way of it, that so there be grounds on each side for gardens.

William Penn, 1682

CLUES
to
American
Garden Styles

David P. Fogle
Catherine Mahan
Christopher Weeks

STARRHILL PRESS
Washington & Philadelphia

Published by Starrhill Press
P.O. Box 32342
Washington, DC 20007

Library of Congress Cataloging in Publication Data

Fogle, David P., 1929-
Clues to American garden styles.
Rev. ed. of: Clues to American gardens. ©1987.

Bibliography: p.62
1. Gardens, American—History. 2. Gardens—United
States—Design—History. 3. Gardens, American—
Identification. 4. Gardens—United States—Identification.
I. Mahan, Catherine, 1947-   . II. Weeks, Christopher,
1950-   . III. Fogle, David P., 1929-   . Clues
to American gardens. IV. Title.
SB457.53.F64   1988   712'.0973   87-18179
ISBN 0-913515-26-4 (pbk.)

Catherine Mahan would like to thank
Anne Coward, Lynn Davidson, Shelley Rentsch, and Susan Wirth
for assisting her with the drawings for this book.

Printed in the United States of America

Revised edition

1 3 5 7 6 4 2

TABLE OF CONTENTS

> And the Lord God planted a garden eastward in Eden
> and there he put the man he had formed.
> from the Book of Genesis

Since earliest times, man has been concerned with the laying out and planting of gardens for utility and pleasure. As the ancient art of gardening progressed through the ages, each epoch left its mark on the next, until tilling the soil has evolved into a rich and varied occupation for professionals and amateurs alike. Indeed, recent studies have shown that today gardening is the most popular hobby in America, far surpassing amateur athletics and the collecting of stamps and coins.

An interpretation of a 16th-century French formal garden appears in a 1604 plan for the settling of an island at the mouth of the St. Croix River off the coast of Maine. Parks—including public gardens—were an integral part of William Penn's 1682 plan for Philadelphia and figure prominently in the layout of other colonial towns such as Williamsburg, Boston, and Savannah. The reconstructed pleasure grounds at Mount Vernon and Monticello attest to the importance of private gardens in the development of the estates of the country's founding fathers. Generally speaking, styles in the northern colonies were based on the informal English concepts of gardening, while many of those in the south were more classically formal. Spanish colonists, settling in Florida and the southwest, designed their gardens according to the horticultural traditions of Iberia.

From these European beginnings, modified by unfamiliar and often severe climates and by the many new plant species discovered here, the art of garden design has developed in this country over the last 300 years into a number of identifiable styles. In this small volume, we have attempted to illustrate and describe these styles for the reader. We have defined "gardening" to mean the purposeful use of plant material, thereby intentionally including not only private gardens, but public gardens, parks, and other public spaces as well. We shall see how Americans' interest in horticulture has grown and developed over several generations and at several different levels of sophistication. We have arranged the garden styles chronologically, based on their first appearance in North America, and have included not only one or two main examples but also, where appropriate, several "clues" to help identify each style. It is important to keep in mind that, while many garden styles reflect the architecture and other arts of their time, the stylistic line of gardens is rarely as clearly drawn as it is in building or painting. Moreover, gardens, made up of living, growing things, continually expand and change. Furthermore, there has always been a tendency, particularly noticeable in large estates built around 1900, to mix many styles in one place, producing exotic mixtures. Longwood Gardens in Chester County, Pennsylvania, and Dumbarton Oaks in Washington, D.C., are two examples of such horticultural eclecticism.

In general, the identifying clues used here are the gardens' shapes, their two-or three-dimensional layouts, the types and characteristics of plant materials, and the non-vegetative ornaments such as statues and fountains and rocks that may be present.

From the beginning, gardens have provided sustenance for the spirit as well as for the body. The authors invite you to use this book to determine the influences on the gardens you see around you, with the realization that many are truly one-of-a-kind, unrelated to any one particular style. We hope that the book, in adding to your knowledge of garden design, will enhance your pleasure and delight—which is, after all, the main purpose of any garden.

David P. Fogle
Catherine Mahan
Christopher Weeks

No occupation is so delightful to me as the culture of the earth, and no culture comparable to that of the garden. . . . But though an old man, I am but a young gardener.

Thomas Jefferson, 1811

8 FARMSTEAD GARDEN

Most people assume that for the first European settlers in America gardening did not mean luxury and beauty—but survival. Those pioneers, after all, had to adapt their old-country practices to a far more demanding and diverse climate than any they had known: it is hard to imagine how great must have been the shock of that first New England winter or Carolina summer. But this assumption needs to be tempered, for it is interesting to find that contemporary descriptions of 17th-century gardens often included many strictly ornamental flowers mixed in among the expected utilitarian plants.

British writer John Josselyn made trips to New England in 1638 and 1663 and recorded the plants he found growing in gardens in and around Boston: "Such Garden Herbs as do thrive there" included "Marygold . . . White Sattan [lunaria], Gilly Flowers [pinks], Hollyhocks, [and] English Roses." In his 1650 *Description of New Netherland*, Adrien van der Donck noted "peonies and hollyhocks . . . crown imperials, white lilies . . . bare dames, violets, marigolds, etc." The famous 1660 map of New Amsterdam, known as the Costello Plan, shows houses surrounded by pleasure gardens laid out along the formal geometric lines then fashionable in Holland.

In the South, and a generation later, Robert Beverley compiled his *History and Present State of Virginia* in which he told how colonists in the Old Dominion took advantage of what grew naturally along the James and Rappahannock rivers. For instance, Beverley admired William Byrd's plantation, Westover, and praised its "Summer House set round with the Indian Honey Suckle, which all the Summer is continually full of sweet flowers, in which [hummingbirds] delight exceedingly."

Nearby, at Bacon's Castle, archaeologists sponsored by the Garden Club of Virginia have uncovered remains of a c.1680 garden that measured 360' x 200' and was divided into six geometric planting beds separated by wide walks. When restored, using period plant material, this will be one of the earliest authentic garden re-creations in the country. (CW)

LOOK FOR:

mixed herbs and flowers
(above, right)

informal layout

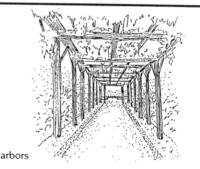

arbors

Mission House, Stockbridge, Massachusetts

paling
and rail
fences

Spanish gardens flourish in Florida, California, and the southwestern parts of the country. While akin to Italian gardens in design, they tend to be more dramatic in the variety and color of their plant materials. Palm and citrus trees, eucalyptus, bougainvillaea, jasmine, and hibiscus are colorful and aromatic features.

Florida and the Southwest were colonized by Spain in the 16th century; St. Augustine, founded in 1565, lays claim to being the oldest city built by white settlers in North America. In the late 16th century, King Philip II of Spain promulgated the Law of the Indies, which established standards for laying out colonial towns, including public plazas and areas of cultivation. It may well be that Spanish gardens were the first examples of European garden design to appear in the New World.

Later gardeners in the Spanish tradition must include Father Junipero Serra and the Franciscan monks, who established 29 missions between San Diego and San Francisco in the 18th century. Father Serra planted the first date palm in America and, with his colleagues, introduced oranges, lemons, figs, grapes, peaches, and pears to the California landscape. The charm of the Spanish garden remains today at these locations.

After a decline in the 19th century, interest in Spanish gardens was revived flamboyantly at the Pan American Exposition at San Diego in 1915. This set off a passion for Spanish or "Mediterranean" style buildings and gardens which continued unabated through the 1930s and, to a lesser degree, to the present time. The gardens are mostly formal and axial, incorporating distant views of sea or mountains, with spacious terraces, patios, walkways, and pools of water. The current trend is to minimize the lush tropical plants, which require care and abundant water, and to focus on desert plants.

A high point in the art of the Spanish garden, with Italian overtones, is the design of La Cuesta Encantada, the William Randolph Hearst estate at San Simeon, California. In St. Augustine, Florida, a simple, authentic Spanish garden has been created at "The Oldest House." (DPF)

LOOK FOR:

flowering vines
and tropical plants

trickling fountains

mosaic paving

cactus and other
desert plants

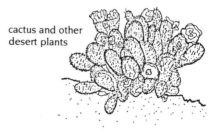

Gonzalez-Alvarez House, "The Oldest House," St. Augustine, Florida

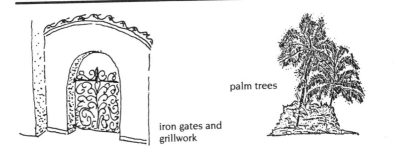

iron gates and grillwork

palm trees

In the deep South, climate and culture combine magnificently to create the courtyard garden, one of North America's finest contributions to the art of urban living. While such gardens appear in Charleston, South Carolina, and Mobile, Alabama, the genre may be at its lush best in New Orleans's famed Vieux Carré.

Everything and everyone in New Orleans braises during that city's nine-month summer. Streets simmer in intense, constant heat, while moisture pours down in monsoon-like thunderstorms. In 1718, the French explorer Bienville chose this steamy site as the location for his new trading post, and for the rest of the 18th century, *La Nouvelle Orléans* prospered as the center of French and Spanish culture in the New World.

These early settlers brought their Old World building forms to Louisiana but quickly modified them to suit the strange subtropical wilderness: deep houses were built flush with the sidewalk with side overhangs for shelter from sun and storms. The front rooms housed stores; the owner and his family retreated to living quarters at the rear, reached from the street by a carriage-way which led through an arched gate back to the residence via a paved courtyard. The courtyard garden's original function was to provide a place for carriages to park. The courtyards were also excellent climate-control devices: their high brick walls and openness allowed builders to create shade-giving galleries along the sides of their living quarters.

Courtyards then evolved into outdoor living rooms—private spaces to enjoy everything from morning café au lait to candlelit cognacs, and the design-conscious French quickly made these once-simple areas decorative by fashioning symmetrical, sharp-lined planting plans. It is probably just as well that the plans were so tidy for this climate would reduce anything less regimented into jungle chaos.

And so the courtyard gardens combine two opposites: orderly designs and rampantly growing plant material. Banana trees give deep shade and

LOOK FOR:

plants such as camellias, kumquats, jasmine, palms, bougainvillaea, magnolias, banana trees, oleanders, water lilies, osmanthus, wisteria, and citrus trees

arched gateways

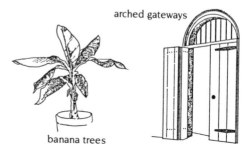

banana trees

soften hard corners; camellia, oleander, azalea, and pomegranate shrubs explode in luxurious color; magnolia, osmanthus, citrus trees, and jasmine vines fill the air with sweetness; fountains splash and drip, adding charming sounds to this highly complex garden system. (CW)

Beauregard-Keyes House, New Orleans, Louisiana

fountains

vine-covered balconies

In colonial America, many wealthy settlers chose to position their houses on the top of a hill. Here they were not only able to enjoy the views and the cooling summer breezes, but they were also above the damp, unhealthy lowland air. Several of these elevated colonists turned their attention to beautifying their hilltop sites by using the natural contours of the land to form "falls gardens"—terraces with allées, walks, and cross-walks leading down from the house to the river or road below. Besides being healthy and scenic, such plans had the further advantage of being fashionable, in that a system of allées would have fit in well with the contemporary formal gardens of Europe that the colonists would have read about or seen on grand tours.

Archaeologists have uncovered such a plan at Carter's Grove, constructed by Burwell Carter along the north bank of the James River in Virginia in about 1760. Almost directly across the James is Brandon, whose falls garden is still evolving today. To arrive at Brandon by boat remains one of the most delightful of American experiences. One steps onto dry land and then begins to climb a centrally placed turf path, up tier after landscaped tier to the welcoming house. The greens of Brandon's terraced garden are of all hues and textures. Boxwood, magnolia, and azalea are evergreen; deciduous green comes from crape myrtle and many kinds of herbaceous perennials.

Baltimore is flanked by two superb 18th-century falls gardens. Around 1790, the Ridgely family began landscaping the grounds around their mansion, Hampton, then in the wilderness but now ringed by suburbs. In one of the largest earth-moving projects then seen in America, they dug and hauled and pushed and piled tons of soil to create three broad terraces off the house's south facade. A generation earlier, and just south of the city, Charles and Margaret Tilghman Carroll, with the help of Phillip Miller's popular 1760 *Gardener's Dictionary*, created their own extensive falls gardens at Mount Clare. The work was thoroughly recorded in landscape paintings and other documents. Mount Clare in its prime formed one of colonial America's most notable house and garden complexes. At one time, one could walk from the main house down a broad allée past five terraces that rolled down to the Carrolls' own docks at the Baltimore harbor. A visitor in 1770 praised Mount Clare, saying that it "stands upon a very High Hill and has a fine view|. . . the whole Plant|ation| seems to be laid out like a Garden." No small statement, for the whole plantation covered more than 2500 acres!

But the most splendid of all terrace gardens, and luckily the best preserved, is Middleton Place in South Carolina. Sculpted by Henry Middleton in 1741 on ancestral acres about 10 miles up the Ashley River from Charleston, this is thought to be the oldest landscaped garden in America. It took Middleton's 100 slaves nine years to construct the 65-

acre pleasure grounds, which include a bowling green, a "mount" (a man-made hill, then the rage in England), parterres and, as a climax, a series of six grassy terraces to connect the main gardens with a pair of "butterfly lakes" at the Ashley's edge. (CW)

Middleton Place, near Charleston, South Carolina

Picturesque gardening came to America by way of Thomas Jefferson. While Minister to France, from 1784 to 1789, Jefferson traveled to England where he was smitten by the English "natural" garden.

What we think of as the English Garden, often called "Britain's greatest contribution to the visual arts," was introduced about 1720 under the multi-talented leadership of the poet Alexander Pope, the artist William Kent, the gardener "Capability" Brown, and the aristocratic patron Richard Boyle, third Earl of Burlington. Kent's theories, popularized by Pope, were intended to create dreamlike parks in which the bewigged English gentry could stroll as through a Poussin painting, possibly spotting a nymph or a satyr coyly gamboling about shady temples, half-hidden in misty vistas. The ideal was perhaps best expressed by Horace Walpole who said he wanted "a garden as elegant and antique as if the Emperor Julian had selected the most pleasing solitude about Daphne to enjoy philosophic retirement."

By the 1780s, when Jefferson was in England, this romantic manner of planting was, after two generations of fertilizing, at its leafy maturity. Entranced, he wrote that this was "a beauty of the very finest order in landscape. Their canvas is of open ground, variegated with clumps of trees distributed with taste."

In 1806, Jefferson was back in America and, while planning his retirement from the burdens of the White House, was mentally re-landscaping Monticello: "The grounds I destine to improve in the style of the English garden." This he did by interspersing tall trees with "clumps of thicket," and by laying a "winding walk surrounding the lawn before the house, with a narrow border of flowers on each side. This would give us abundant room for a great variety." He heightened this sense of "variety" by placing many ornamental whimsies such as temples and pavilions about the grounds. These sophisticated frivolities were intended to be seen from afar—"vistas to very interesting objects"—and were to act as civilized counterpoints to the "wild" plantings.

LOOK FOR:

lakes and streams

clumps of trees and shrubs

rambling paths

Jefferson was ahead of his time, and the American romantic garden idea lay dormant until 1841 when A. J. Downing published his *Treatise on Landscape Gardening*. This text nicely coincided with the romantic era in the other arts, and Downing's theories became immensely popular. He wrote that the "picturesque school" ought to produce "a certain spiritual irregularity." He advocated dark-foliaged evergreens to create "thickets, glades, and underwood, as in nature." These were to be set off in hue by purple and copper beeches. Downing grouped his many-toned trees in clumps, broken by a few "elegant specimens." These rounded forms were accompanied by undulating paths and the curved banks of meandering streams, and all recall Jefferson's Monticello with its "great variety." (CW)

Blithewood, Dutchess County, New York
(from A.J. Downing's *Treatise on Landscape Gardens*)

pavilions,
garden houses,
temples

Eighteenth-century poet and hymnist William Cowper wrote in his book, *The Garden*, "Who loves a garden loves a greenhouse too." This was certainly true of America's colonial elite who appear to have been fascinated by greenhouses (interchangeably called hothouses and orangeries). In 1767, Elizabeth Tayloe of Mount Airy in Virginia married Edward Lloyd IV of Wye in Maryland; both their plantations had hothouses where oranges and lemons flourished. Lloyd went in for even more exotic fruit, it seems, for he owned a copy of John Abercrombie's 1789 publication, *The Hot-House Gardener, or the General Cultivation of the Pine-Apple*. Across the Chesapeake Bay, Charles Carroll, Barrister, had an orangerie at his country seat, Mount Clare, near Baltimore, and ordered a thermometer for it in 1760. Mrs. Carroll's first cousin, Tench Tilghman, was a long-time friend of George Washington, who was himself a keen hothouse gardener. When Washington was building his orangerie at Mount Vernon in 1784, he asked Tench Tilghman to go to Mount Clare and "give a short description of the Green-house at Mrs. Carroll's . . . the dimensions . . . what kind of floor . . . how high from the floor to the bottom of the window frame . . . whether the heat is carried by flues," and so on.

Farther north, wealthy Philadelphians were building themselves greenhouses along the banks of the Schuykill River. John Penn, William's son, planted an elaborate garden at Springettsburg where, according to a 1754 letter, he raised "oranges, limes, limons [sic], and citrons," crops which suggest some sort of hothouse. Nearby was The Hills, William Morris's country seat. Morris is known today as the financier of the American Revolution, but in his day he was famous as the first man in Philadelphia to grow lemons. So well known were his tangy fruits that his estate was renamed Lemon Hill to honor his hothouse successes.

Rather than separate, specially heated structures, other colonial/federal period houses had south-facing rooms built into the main fabric of the building. These provided shelter for tender flowering plants such as oleander and hibiscus, and for such important culinary plants as bay

---

LOOK FOR:

exotic collections
of tender plants

potted citrus trees

(*Laurus nobilis*). Extant examples include Tudor Place in Georgetown, Washington, D.C., built in 1815 for Thomas Peter, and Monticello, where Thomas Jefferson kept tubs of his beloved *Mimosa nilotica*, which he called "the most delicious shrub in the world."

Conservatories were integral features of Victorian gardening, and no mansion was considered complete without its Palm Room. These glazed spaces were also recognized as excellent teaching devices: one of the earliest academic greenhouses is the 1880 Lyman Plant House at Smith College in Northampton, Massachusetts.

Prefabricated by such firms as Lord and Burnham, greenhouses continue to provide hours of pleasure to gardeners in our own time. (CW)

Orangerie, Wye House, Talbot County, Maryland

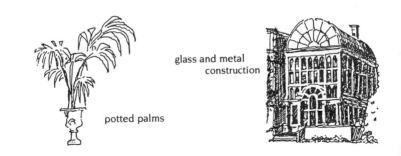

glass and metal construction

potted palms

"Man longs, amidst the lines and angles, and the artificial ornaments of even a palace, to behold the unmeasured variety of nature." So wrote the South Carolinian Charles Fraser in his *Charleston Sketchbook*, 1796-1806. Fraser, a frequent guest at the great rice plantations of the South Carolina and Georgia coasts, was also an artist of some skill, and his paintings and sketches of what he saw along the Ashley and Cooper rivers and Goose Creek reveal how the tidal aristocrats had, by taking advantage of their terrain and climate, created an indigenous style of gardening that remains unique, romantic, and of an unearthly beauty.

Ante-bellum Charleston glistened as the cultural capital of the South, leading the way in architecture, furniture making, painting, and especially gardening. Travelers marveled at Low Country horticulture: there was the happily-named Dr. Garden who, in the 1760s, imported plants from as far away as China and whom Linnaeus honored in the name *Gardenia*, just as the good doctor's neighbor, Joel Poinsett, is remembered each Christmas for his plant introduction, *Poinsettia*; another near neighbor, André Michaux, became the first person in this country to grow camellias when he planted four slips at Middleton Place in 1786.

It is not the plant specialist, however, but the lay of the land and water that gives Low Country gardens their haunting appeal. A sense of majesty fills the soul as one walks along mile after hazy mile of informal, shady paths that wander amid moss-hung oaks and cypresses, skirting inky, opalescent lakes, and paralleling streams so sluggish they seem to be finished in black lacquer. Even the names of the places are evocative—who can doubt what is growing at Magnolia or Cypress Gardens?

The English novelist John Galsworthy strolled through Magnolia Gardens and left bewitched. He wrote that although he had seen thousands of gardens, "none in the world is so beautiful as this . . . nothing so free and gracious, so lively and wistful, nothing so richly coloured, yet so ghostlike, exists planted by the sons of man. It is a kind of Paradise . . . a miraculously enchanted wilderness." (CW)

LOOK FOR:

expansive scale

azaleas and camellias, informally planted

live oaks

Cypress Gardens, near Charleston, South Carolina

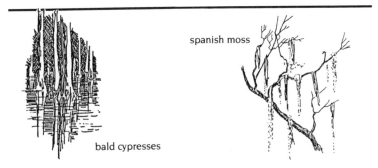

spanish moss

bald cypresses

One thinks of Victorian architecture as being enthusiastically larger than life. If that generalization is true of buildings, it is just as valid for gardens. This—the mid-19th century—was the era of exaggeration, of the "great effect." Believing that nothing succeeds like excess, many gardeners, in private plots and in parks, became keen bedders-out. To this end, they revived the *parterre* of the French Renaissance garden. A parterre, etymologically akin to "parquet," is an intricately designed flower bed of sinuous shape, perhaps best seen from above.

For dramatic effect, these huge curving beds were filled with hundreds or even thousands of plants of a single variety and color. These would be replaced according to the season: masses of monochromatic tulips would give way to dahlias or cannas or salvia (preferably red) or geraniums or coleus; these in turn would be replaced by chrysanthemums until the first hard frost put a blackened end to it all.

Today, bedding out is usually practiced by municipal, state, and federal governments, and in parks throughout America one can come upon a mass of blazing gold or crimson glowing in the summer sun. An outstanding example of this style may be seen at the International Peace Garden in Salt Lake City where scores of flowering plants have been arranged to spell out GOD BLESS AMERICA. (CW)

A Victorian Summer House, New Jersey

For hundreds of years, northern Europeans viewed the Alps as a forbidding barrier between themselves and the delights of Italy. In the mid-19th century, however, romantics began to look at these mountains—and craggy hills in general—as things of great beauty. With this reversal in sensibilities came a delight in Alpine gardens, or "rockeries."

Rock gardens quickly found favor in America, for they not only suited our aesthetic sense but were practical as well. Today, many building lots have outcroppings of stone and rock, while many others have steep slopes and banks. All these features suit rock gardening, a form of horticulture that allows the gardener to work with, rather than against, his land. In the words of garden historian Peter Coats, a rock garden "should be on a slope—for drainage is all important for all rock plants. It should lie—like the foothills of the Alps—open to the sky. There should be no spreading trees to deprive the garden's denizens of a moment's sunshine."

Effective rock gardeners are basically ecologists, reproducing, in a small space, several different climatic conditions—deep pockets of rich earth for miniature bulbs, moist areas for ferns, and shallow, gritty spots for sturdy plants such as candytuft, heathers, and various sedums. (CW)

A Rock Garden, Ann Arbor, Michigan

American interest in French garden design, apparent in the early days of the new republic, was stimulated by France's participation in the American Revolution on the side of the colonists. The 1791 plan for the new capital city of Washington, by French engineer Major Pierre L'Enfant, was based on the work of landscape architect Le Notre at Versailles in 1660. Gardens in the American South were influenced by French botanist André Michaux who came to Charleston in 1786 to collect plant specimens for the French government. The design of formal Charleston gardens, with their axial paths, geometric flower beds, walls, and gates, reflects the French tradition.

French-style gardens are distinguished by their horizontality, corresponding to the general flatness of the French countryside. Long allées lined with clipped trees or hedges are characteristic, as are pools, fountains, urns, statuary, and constructions of trellis and lattice or *treillage*. French gardens are often done in the "grand manner," an approach shown at Biltmore, the French chateau built in 1896 by George Vanderbilt near Asheville, North Carolina. This project combined the talents of two of the country's foremost designers, William Morris Hunt and Frederick Law Olmsted.

French monarchical grandeur appealed to the new American millionaires of the late 19th and early 20th centuries. It is exemplified by the gardens at Dumbarton Oaks in Washington, D.C., and at the Aldred estate at Glen Cove on Long Island, an expression of the *ferme ornée*, the sort of ornamental farm created by Marie Antoinette at Versailles. French gardens were copied in the 1920s, particularly in affluent suburban developments, to complement a fashion for adapting various French architectural styles to public and private buildings. The formality, geometry, and impressive orderliness of the French garden is in sharp contrast to the romantic English tradition which sought to understand and enhance the

LOOK FOR:

shallow, reflecting pools (above, right)

terraces

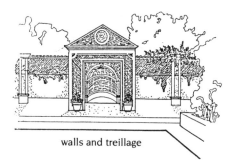

walls and treillage

qualities of the natural environment for man's enjoyment. The French garden, with its careful shaping of shrubs and trees to conform to intricate geometric designs, manifests the triumph of man over nature. (DPF)

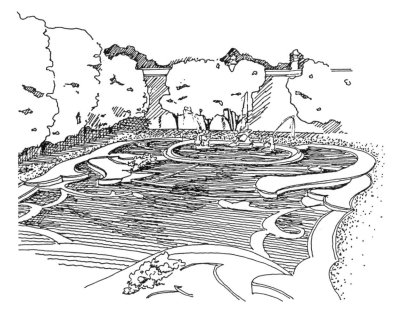

Pool at Dumbarton Oaks, Washington, D.C.

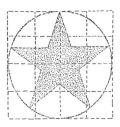

flower designs in colors

flat, geometric designs or "parterres"

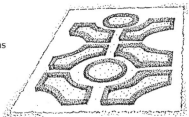

The Italian garden is situated ideally on a sunny southern slope where it can be terraced into various levels connected by stairways and paths. It will often incorporate such garden ornaments as gazebos, pergolas, and trellises and will be further embellished by sculptural fountains and pools, statuary, urns, and balustrades. Multi-colored paving and mosaic work are sometimes used.

A fine Italian garden is found at Maymont near Richmond, Virginia. In 1907, a Richmond firm, Noland and Baskervill, was hired to create an Italian garden for the estate. The garden is a long rectangle with an east-west orientation on a south hillside overlooking the James River. Three levels accommodate a formal garden, a promenade and belvedere, and a lower terrace. One enters under a wisteria-draped pergola which terminates at a domed garden house. From here one descends to the lower garden or enters the formal garden on axis with a fountain and pool. Levels are divided by granite walls decorated with large marble urns planted with flowers. The stairs to the lower garden are on either side of a "chain fountain" cascading down the hill through a chain of pools.

Leading proponents of Italian garden design in America were architect Charles Platt who designed the Sprague garden in Brookline, Massachusetts, and landscape gardener Beatrix Farrand, whose biography lists as her models the "sixteenth and seventeenth century Italian villas and their gardens." A book by Farrand's aunt, Edith Wharton, did much to popularize the style. A superb example of an Italian water garden may be seen at Longwood Gardens in Chester County, Pennsylvania. Later, as the American lifestyle became more casual, the intricately designed and carefully tended Italian garden declined in popularity.

LOOK FOR:

classical garden
structures
(above, right)

geometric
pools of water

clipped evergreen hedges

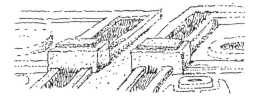

While Italian and French gardens may appear similar in design, differences are usually topographical. French designs are two-dimensional; Italian are multi-level on irregular sites. (DPF)

Charles H. Sprague Garden, Brookline, Massachusetts

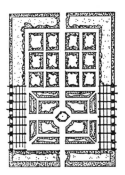

rectangular design

Italian cypress trees

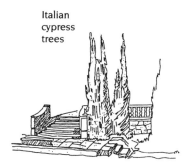

multi-level terraces, stairs and balustrades

In contrast to earlier gardens, which were oases of civilization in the wilderness, urban parks of the latter half of the 19th century offered natural scenes surrounded by the city of man-made objects, noise, and monotonous views.

Major figures in the development of these urban parks were Andrew Jackson Downing who designed the Mall for the nation's capital in 1851 and Frederick Law Olmsted who, with the aid of Calvert Vaux, designed Central Park in New York. Their view, as expressed by Olmsted, was that city parks should provide "relief from too insistently man-made surroundings of civilized life." Peripheral plantings were intended to block off sights and sounds of surrounding urban development. Irregular vistas of natural landscaping were to be a relief from the geometry of city streets. Open spaces, as either plazas or meadows, were provided for people to meet, to walk, and to play. Footpaths and bridle paths wandered through woodland settings.

Although city parks of this period might appear to be left in their natural state, they were in fact laid out by careful design according to rigorous

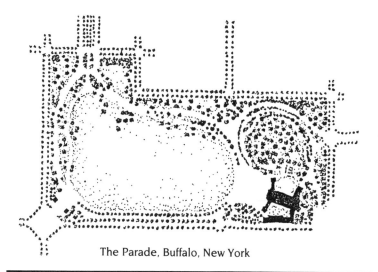

The Parade, Buffalo, New York

LOOK FOR:

natural surroundings

informal groupings
of trees and shrubs

winding roads and paths

lakes, and open
meadowlike spaces

standards. In creating Central Park, some 20,800 barrels of dynamite were used to blast away bedrock in order to form its hills, lakes, and meadows, and over half a million cubic yards of topsoil were brought in to encourage the growth of the 166,000 trees and shrubs planted by the end of 1862.

Olmsted's conception of the city park as representing the natural environment is still a valid basis for park design: the prototype, Central Park, is one of the most successful examples, even today. Its major concept of interspersing land and water, hill and dale, has been widely copied, as has the idea of separating pedestrian and motor traffic. Similar designs were made by the Olmsted firm for the cities of Newark, Buffalo, Albany, Hartford, Chicago, Montreal, Detroit, and Louisville. Prospect Park in Brooklyn, Fairmount Park in Philadelphia, Druid Hill Park in Baltimore, and Golden Gate Park in San Francisco demonstrate the guiding principle of urban park design—the introduction of nature's charms into the built environment. (DPF)

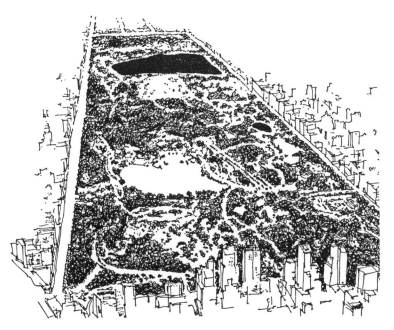

Central Park, New York City

Americans have been entranced by Japanese gardening traditions and principles ever since Admiral Perry "opened up" the Land of the Rising Sun in 1853.

Reverence for nature runs strongly throughout Japan's history, manifesting itself perhaps most clearly in the Japanese love of gardening. The Japanese have turned *ikebana* (a school of flower arranging) into an aesthetic science, and nearly all Japanese homes have a *bonsai* (meaning not only dwarfed trees but entire, perfect, miniature landscapes shaped by sand, moss, stones, and water) in a place of honor in the family *tokonoma*, or shrine. Indoors and out, Japanese gardening is imbued with the spirit of Zen Buddhism and is controlled by a highly complex system wherein each feature has a specific place, significance, and role.

American gardeners who have attempted to emulate the Japanese and their gardens have taken note of the two basic types of Japanese landscape: Hira-niwa (level lands) and Tsuki-yama (high lands). Tsuki-yama have been especially well received in America, perhaps because to western eyes they have more obvious variety and interest, containing, as they often do, mountains, hills, bridges, islands, stones, lanterns, trees, and water. This last feature is indispensable to any Japanese garden, and even dry gardens suggest water by means of sand raked in wavy patterns to symbolize the flow of a stream.

The treatment of stones hints at the intricacy of Japanese gardening thought. There is the familiar *Shiyu-go-Seki* (Guardian Stone), tall and upright, chosen for its sentinel appearance. The *Taki-ishi* (Cliff Stone) is intended to act as a support and companion for the Guardian Stone and is placed at the head of a waterfall. The *Getsu-in-Seki* (Moon Stone) provides solitude. Other stones with special meanings include the Worship Stone, the Water Fowl Stone, the Stone of Easy Rest, the Amusement Seat Stone, the Seat of Honor Stone, the Shoe-Removing Stone, and the Stone of Obeisance.

LOOK FOR:

symbolic stones
and water

bonsai

tea houses

arched bridges

Simple Japanese gardens are called *So*, gardens of intermediate complexity are *Gyo*, and *Shin* are the most involved of all. Few Westerners can ever begin to understand the subtle and complex symbolism in even the simplest Japanese garden. But certainly we can visit such places as the Japanese Garden in George Washington Park, Portland, Oregon, or Brookside Gardens in Maryland, to admire their tranquillity and the beautiful integration of their many parts. (CW)

Tea House, Brookside Gardens, Wheaton, Maryland

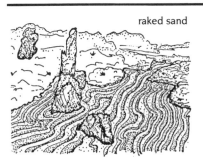

raked sand

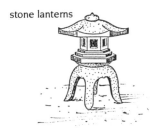

stone lanterns

In South Carolina in the mid-18th century, newly widowed Martha Logan found herself in charge of a plantation near Charleston. Here she sold seeds and plants and compiled what may have been the first American publication on the kitchen garden, *Directions for Managing a Kitchen Garden every month of the year Done by a Lady*.

The traditional kitchen garden might have covered an acre or more, been tended by a gardener or two, and supplied the house with a full range of edibles. Today, although considerably reduced in size in both urban and suburban settings, and cared for by the householder, the kitchen garden retains its essential character.

Ideally, it is adjacent to or easily accessible from the house. Beds are long and narrow for easy cultivation; soil is well-drained and consists of a rich loam to a depth of about two feet. Boundary walls keep deer, rabbits, and other garden raiders out of the garden and can provide, on the south-facing interior side, a surface for a lean-to greenhouse. The plan may include a shed for storage of cultivating tools. Paths of grass, gravel, brick, or stone may be laid out for good access to the house, the water supply, and the areas to be tended. If space allows, these paths may be lined with herbaceous borders or cutting beds with the vegetables behind. The large kitchen garden recreated at Mount Vernon is surrounded by a board fence and laid out in a traditional scheme of rectilinear paths and geometrical beds in which vegetables and flowers are planted in straight rows. Today, organic gardeners and those more informally inclined may mix vegetables with marigolds, zinnias, and other cutting flowers in masses rather than rows.

While a kitchen garden may be aesthetically pleasing, its primary purpose is to provide a ready supply of vegetables and fruits to the kitchen.

Plan of the Kitchen Garden, Mount Vernon, Virginia

It will contain herbs and such regularly used food plants as lettuce, tomatoes, onions, and peppers. Even the smallest space can accommodate a dwarf fruit tree, espaliered perhaps on a sunny wall. The current interest in the culinary arts and exotic foods has spawned a wide variety of available edible plants and a wealth of mail-order seed catalogs from which to obtain them.

Based on the farmstead garden of colonial days, the kitchen garden has been a constant adjunct to the American home. Its utility, aesthetic appeal, and rewards to the amateur gardener remain unchanged. (DPF)

A Small Kitchen Garden of the 1980s

LOOK FOR:

wall, fence, or hedge enclosures	espaliered fruit trees
rectilinear layouts	borders
narrow beds for easy cultivation	vegetables and flowers in rows
small greenhouse	staked plants

The American city, by the end of the 19th century, had become a victim of the Industrial Revolution, blighted by pollution, slum housing, and railroads. In response, the World Columbian Exposition in Chicago in 1893 inaugurated the City Beautiful movement, reviving principles of classicism in building and landscape design.

The Ecole des Beaux-Arts in Paris was the training ground for practitioners of what became known as the Beaux Arts style, the architectural expression of the City Beautiful. The style was based on forms from the Greek and Roman classical periods and from the Italian Renaissance. Landscape design reflected this style with emphasis upon formalism, geometry, and axial arrangements of paths, trees, and gardens. Another influence on the City Beautiful movement came from Paris where Baron Haussmann, an Austrian engineer, had designed grand avenues and plazas for the city, under the auspices of Napoleon III.

The Chicago Fair sparked a nationwide movement to create civic centers, boulevards, and city parks along the classical lines found in Paris, Rome, and Vienna. The pace was set in the nation's capital where a Senate-appointed commission, which included Daniel Burnham, architect of the Chicago exposition, and Frederick Law Olmsted, Jr., set about to replace the existing romantic English garden Mall design with one of classical symmetry. The attraction of the classical design was not foreign to the city: it was in the tradition of the original design for Washington planned by the French engineer Pierre L'Enfant in 1791.

The City Beautiful movement with its Beaux Arts component affected central city design across the country. New public building complexes were built, set in formal parks or gardens; plans for affluent suburbs in growing cities came under the spell of the movement, with private houses designed to sit like jewels in gardens composed of geometric,

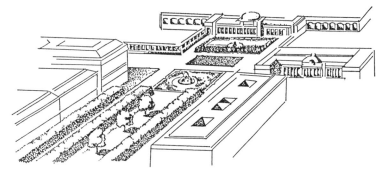

Civic Center, Cleveland, Ohio

two-dimensional shapes, punctuated with fountains, pergolas, and stairways.

In response to the motor age, broad tree-lined boulevards became an important feature of the City Beautiful movement. The Benjamin Franklin Parkway in Philadelphia, El Paseo in Kansas City, and Lakeshore Drive in Chicago are fine examples. (DPF)

Palace of Fine Arts, San Francisco, California

LOOK FOR:

adjacent Beaux Arts buildings

reflecting pools and
high rising fountains
(above)

large scale designs

rectilinear and axial plantings

malls and boulevards

"Expansive" well describes gardening in the era of great industrial fortunes before the advent of the income tax. One historian has dubbed the score of years on either side of 1900 as "the Country Place Era," when the economically secure were discovering the charms of Long Island's North Shore, Philadelphia's Main Line, the Berkshire Mountains, Grosse Pointe in Michigan, and the Peninsula south of San Francisco. In these and other favored enclaves, America's rich sought to escape from the brusque industrial sources of their wealth into an idealized countryside.

Fiske Kimball, in his classic article, "The American Country House," (1919) noted the rapid increase in the number of millionaires after 1890 and "the great wave of renewed love of out-of-door life and of nature which swept over America in the last years of the nineteenth century and the opening years of the twentieth." These millionaires didn't necessarily want real country places—they required too much work—but they did want the illusion of country life. Designing their 20-acre mini-paradises was a demanding task, for the grounds had to seem to flow, to go on forever. In addition, several things were de rigueur: a tennis court, a sweep of lawn, a swimming pool, a small orchard underplanted with daffodils, separate vegetable and cutting gardens, perhaps a greenhouse for winter blossoms, a dock if on the water, possibly a stable and some bridle paths. These features couldn't overlap, actually or visually, and the task of placement produced several skilled landscape artists, many of whom are now getting their just recognition from a scholarly community that for many years suffered from severe inverse snobbery.

One of the most notable of the group is Beatrix Jones Farrand, who deserves a paragraph of her own. Born in New York in 1872, she studied under Charles Sargent at the Arnold Arboretum and in 1899 was one of eleven founders of the American Society of Landscape Architects. Although perhaps best known for her campus projects at Princeton, Yale, and Oberlin, her residential work was also of immense influence, and her scores of commissions span the continent from Bar Harbor to Pasadena.

LOOK FOR:

grand scale

terraces

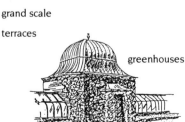
greenhouses

expansive vistas

But, in the eyes of many, her most notable achievement, created for Mr. and Mrs. Robert Woods Bliss, was Dumbarton Oaks, in Georgetown, Washington, D.C. Here she worked more or less continuously from 1922 until her death in 1959. (CW)

Chapin Garden, Grosse Pointe Farms, Michigan

walls and gates

swimming pools

This is what comes to most of us, in our mind's eye, when we hear the word "garden:" visions of long rows of gaily colored hardy perennials blooming their sweet-scented heads off for six or seven months.

But it hasn't always been thus. In fact, the herbaceous border is a relatively new invention. While no one seems to know just who first used the phrase, now so familiar, the gardener who popularized the idea of the herbaceous border can be identified. He was William Robinson, who wrote in his *The English Flower Garden*, (1883): "We now come to the flowers that are worthy of a place in gardens . . . a simple border has been the first expression of flower gardening, and as there is no arrangement of flowers more graceful, varied, or more capable of giving delight, and none so easily adapted to almost every kind of garden, some ideas of the various kinds of borders of hardy flowers . . . deserves our first consideration."

William Robinson's name may be unfamiliar to many weekend gardeners, but another late-Victorian tiller of the English soil grows in fame and gathers in more legions of admirers every year: Gertrude Jekyll, a name that will forever be linked with the herbaceous border. Around 1900, Jekyll and other sensitive gardeners grew weary of the then prevailing system of bedding-out and rebelled at what they perceived as a graceless use of plant material. Jekyll expressed it in her 1929 memoirs: "Fifty years ago, when the bedding out of tender plants for a summer display was the general garden practice, if any thought was given to arranging [the plants] for colour, it was to produce the crudest and most garish effects, such as a round bed of vivid scarlet geraniums with a border of blue lobelia." For Miss Jekyll, "all that concerns the planting of our gardens is . . . the better use of colour."

The herbaceous border is, basically, a strip of garden of varying width and length (Gertrude Jekyll's measured 14′ x 200′), ideally facing south with a wall of old brick or of mellow-colored stone behind and a path of stone and/or grass in front. Within the border, the placement of individual plants, paying close attention to their size, spread, leaf texture, flower color, and period of bloom, was a dead serious concern.

For most of us today, a Jekyll border would be an economic impossibility: the planting would cost thousands and the maintenance even more. But the herbaceous border remains the ideal of many American gardeners. So, the necessary reduction in scale has led to the invention of many variations on the theme. Perhaps the most interesting is the single color garden. Jekyll, again, was among the first to indulge in such fancies:

LOOK FOR:

continuous bloom, variety of leaf textures, ordered scale and color

"Suddenly entering the gold garden, even on the dullest day, will be like coming into sunshine." A generation later, V. Sackville-West made her now legendary white garden at Sissinghurst, and in this country people like Harvey Ladew were busily planning their gardens of white or pink, gold or blue. Merely as a guide, this is what Ladew planted in his white garden north of Baltimore: dogwood, stewartia, several varieties of white chrysanthemums, impatiens, tulips, nicotiana, cimicifuga, lily-of-the-valley, snapdragons, narcissus, hosta, viburnum, philadelphus, clethra, and lilac. As can be seen, such a list provides for many months of blossom, continuous textural interest, and a wide variety of plant height. (CW)

White Flower Farm, Litchfield, Connecticut

The first use of the word "parkway" as it is known today was made by Frederick Law Olmsted who, with Calvert Vaux, designed New York City's Central Park. Here in Central Park he developed the innovative concept of separating roads for vehicles and pedestrians for the greater pleasure and safety of both. But it was not until their 1870 design for a boulevard running east to the plaza of Prospect Park in Brooklyn that the term "parkway" was applied. Originally named Jamaica Parkway, it soon became known as Eastern Parkway. The creation of this roadway brought about a new understanding of road design as an integral part of park design. Parkways were designed from then on as traveled ways *within* parks.

With the completion of New York City's Bronx River Parkway after World War I, the parkway as a uniquely American roadway type had emerged. It was a road designed for pleasure vehicles only (no trucks) and for leisurely driving at low speeds (originally 30 mph). It was further distinguished by having a right-of-way wide enough to maintain natural features and to prevent encroaching development. The road alignment was a series of gentle curves flowing over the existing topography, and adjacent landscaping was carried out with native plant materials chosen to harmonize with the local vegetation. The parkway was further characterized by allowing limited access to the roadway and by restricting signing and billboards.

The success of the Bronx River Parkway brought about the formation of the Westchester County Park Commission which acquired and developed lands for parks and parkways. This Commission succeeded in developing one of the most exemplary systems of parks and linking parkways in the country. Among these are the Saw Mill River, the Hutchinson River, the Briarcliff-Peekskill, and Cross County Parkways, all in the vicinity of New York City.

As the parkway systems grew, another development came about which seems so commonplace today it is hard to imagine how recently it emerged: that of the divided highway. The Taconic Parkway along the Hudson River in New York State was one of the first such roads laid out with a central divider. This required less grading of the earth in road construction and consequently allowed for the retention of more of the existing vegetation. While the early median strips were only 15' or 20' wide, the advantages of independent alignments were soon seen, and parkways began to develop with broad median strips.

In 1929, the Bureau of Public Roads built the Mount Vernon Memorial Parkway linking Washington, D.C., and Mount Vernon, Virginia. Construction of the Merritt Parkway in Connecticut soon followed. Then in 1931 the first federal parkway, Skyline Drive, was built atop the Blue Ridge Mountains in Virginia, in the area soon to become Shenandoah National Park. Skyline Drive is extended to the south by the Blue Ridge Parkway through Great Smoky Mountains National Park, making one of the most spectacular expanses of mountain parkway in the country. Skyline Drive is largely located on the crests of the mountains, affording extensive views, while the Blue Ridge Parkway travels up and down the the terrain and is consequently the more interesting to experience.

Expansion of the parkway system continued, creating the Colonial Parkway between Jamestown and Yorktown, Virginia, and the Natchez Trace which follows an old Indian trail from Nashville, Tennessee, to Natchez, Mississippi.

Much of the knowledge gained in the development of the nation's parkways was put to use in the interstate highway system. Interstates, however, differ from parkways in a major way: they are designed for the rapid movement of all types of vehicles, in contrast to the leisurely pleasure driving of cars on the parkways. Because of the high speeds, the adjacent landscape is perceived much more rapidly, and detail is lost. The clumps of flowering trees and shrubs seen along parkways would not be appreciated traveling at interstate speeds. By contrast, the roads of continuing curvature laid lightly on the land require the constant attention of the driver who is amply rewarded with the pleasant sensation of moving through a natural landscape of which he or she is an integral part. (CM)

Wilbur Cross Parkway, Fairfield County, Connecticut

Faced with an increasingly ugly industrialized world in the late 19th century, many men and women of artistic temperament turned their collective backs on the dreary present in favor of the perceived beauty, tradition, and peace of the past. Whether or not such a reaction was appropriate is not the issue. The point is that as the 20th century has clanked and blasted along, bringing with it a brace of world wars, unprecedented economic depressions, and since 1945 the threat of nuclear annihilation, an escape to the security of the past has not lost one whit of appeal, and historic re-creations have become a virtual growth industry.

Methods and techniques have made bold advances in this century, and scholarship has more than kept up with demand. The earliest re-creations were based on somewhat sketchy information and on documentation such as paintings and letters, rarely very detailed. Thus, landscaping efforts tended to use what was viscerally attractive and "old looking." The results, if not always accurate, were nevertheless romantic and beautiful.

William Paca House and Garden, Annapolis, Maryland

Since World War II, and especially within the past 20 years, such conjectural historicism, while pleasant enough, has been replaced by an almost burning desire for intellectual honesty. This in turn has been made possible by improved methods of scientific research: archaeologists in particular have developed sophisticated techniques to discover the most elusive minutiae about our ancestors' gardening habits. The result is that today a visit to places as varied as the "medieval" Cloisters or the "colonial" Paca gardens ought to cure the most virulent sufferer of what Noel Coward called "Twentieth Century Blues." (CW)

The Cloisters, New York City

In 1955, Christopher Isherwood described the Eisenhower era as a time of "peaceprosperityexpandingeconomypermanentboom." Given an apparently eternally secure economy, men and women shed their gray flannel suits long enough to make thousands of gardens on quarter-acre plots in subdivisions from coast to coast. These gardens share many aesthetic features with the tract houses they were intended to complement and form a style as instantly recognizable as any other widely practiced manner of horticulture. Scorned by the intelligentsia of the time, this was gardening for the ordinary citizen—a truly vernacular approach to horticulture. And if these gardens seem stereotypical in the 1980s, it is good to consider that a past generation, whose parents were keen bedders-out, rebelled and created the herbaceous border. One waits to see what the next vernacular gardening style will be.

Curiously, the most interesting phenomenon of this period has received little comment, although its long-term importance seems immense. Lawns were the sine qua non of 1950s gardens: blue grass ruled the country. To bring about the never-ending grassy lots, whole forests were felled and vast marshes filled in throughout the North and Midwest, while in the arid Southwest, mammoth irrigation projects made former deserts green. This, in effect, transformed the ecological make-up of America by creating millions of contiguous acres of savannah. In addition, large percentages of these small lots were given over to the needs of the family car. The ultimate implications of this prairie-ing and paving of the American landscape have yet to be seen.

The gardens of the '50s and '60s were a product of mass-circulation magazines, and of television, which beamed the adventures of "Father Knows Best" families and their better homes and gardens to millions of viewers each week. It may be said that the style reached its apotheosis in "I Love Lucy" when the Ricardos moved from Manhattan to Westport, Connecticut: here in suburban splendor Lucy could turn her considerable talents to back yard horticulture and could scheme, not of ways to make a career in show business, but of ways to raise prize-winning tulips and neatly mown grass for the local garden club competition.

LOOK FOR:

perimeter and
foundation plantings
(above, right)

outdoor lights

For Lucy, and for the millions who followed her, that tidy green lawn was of paramount importance, not only because it was thought to look nice but also because it gave a place for webbed lawn furniture and a spot where the family could indulge in outdoor barbecuing. "Patios," closer to the house, were popular for similar reasons. Foundation planting was a must, and the shrubs—yew, azalea, and arborvitae—had to be as tightly clipped as the grass was closely mowed. Privet hedges—firmly pruned—provided some, but not too much, privacy. Sometimes vegetables were grown in separate plots, but such practical gardening was not generally favored: it recalled the '40s Victory Gardens and, besides, that's what the new supermarkets were for. Instead, any spots of worked earth, most often perimeter beds around the edges of the lot, would be given over to newly hybridized, scentless roses or to market-packed annuals purchased at any one of thousands of identical garden centers.

Such gardening wasn't new to the 1950s. Back in the '20s, suburban gardens were literally packaged and sold as units, along with mail order houses, by Sears Roebuck & Co. It was the scale of the postwar gardening effort that set it apart. (CW)

The American Dream House and Garden c. 1955

furniture for outdoor living

foundation planting

Those fortunate enough to possess a plot of ground by the sea and who wish to make a garden have two general choices: either they can turn the sand to loam and garden as if they were back home, or they can respect the maritime environment and choose plants suitable to it. While neither type of garden is "correct" or "incorrect," this discussion will focus on the latter approach.

Most seaside plants tend to have leaves that are extreme, either extremely thick, fleshy, and water-retentive, such as the sedums, or extremely thin and needlelike, such as pines, rosemary, and broom. Rugosa roses are pleasantly ubiquitous as are sun-loving geraniums and, along the New England coast, hollyhocks and big purple hydrangeas.

The point in choosing maritime plants for a maritime environment is that one goes to the ocean to relax, after all, so one might as well have plants that don't require a lot of fuss. Other fairly maintenance-free flora for the desiccating environment of sun, sand, wind, and spray include sea buckthorn (*Hippophae rhamnoides*), beach plum (*Prunus maritima*; necessary for that quintessential beach product, beach plum jelly), Montauk daisy (*Chrysanthemum nipponicum*), and Monterey pine (*Pinus radiata*)—wonderful on the Pacific coast and from Delaware south on the Atlantic. Grasses are almost mandatory, and sea oats (*Uniola paniculata*) is as good in the Southeast as its cousin, *U. latiflora*, is in the Northeast.

Most annuals will grow well if they are watered regularly (a chore the vacationer may wish to avoid); zinnias and marigolds stand out as particularly good choices. It is also possible to have a seaside garden of herbaceous perennials: daylilies, gaillardia, potentilla, and lavender all merit consideration.

Finally, because one wishes to dine well off local produce like fresh fish and just-picked vegetables, it is satisfying to note that most culinary herbs, both annual and perennial, thrive along our coasts. Sage and mint, basil and thyme, tarragon and parsley, all will please the palate and perfume the air. (CW)

LOOK FOR:

windswept pines

A Garden in Siasconset, Nantucket Island, Massachusetts

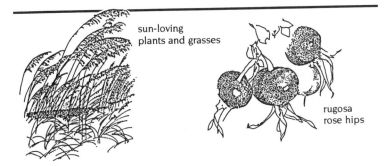

sun-loving
plants and grasses

rugosa
rose hips

This might well be thought of as the logical—if extreme—outcome of the principles that guided the natural garden revolution in the 18th century. While those early natural gardeners were somewhat tempered by Alexander Pope's famous horticultural dictum, "Not nature bare, but nature methodized," today's wildflower enthusiasts prefer their nature bare as they seek to maintain, or to re-create, a habitat for plants that seems as pure as pre-fall Eden.

On a large scale, this sometimes results in azalea-filled pine forests, as at Winterthur in Delaware or the 14-acre Woodland Garden at Bayou Bend in Houston. On a small scale, the challenge is even greater; it usually means creating a "wild" environment in a suburban space and then finding plants that will be happy in it. Note that wild does not mean haphazard. Plantings may look spontaneous, but everything must be tightly controlled. Nineteenth-century English landscape gardener Gertrude Jekyll, in *Wood and Garden*, warns that "azaleas should never be placed among or even in sight of rhododendrons. Though both enjoy a moist peat soil and have a near botanical relationship, they are incongruous in appearance and impossible to group together for colour."

While it is useless to attempt to make an all-inclusive list of "wild" plants, a few species might be suggested either because they will grow in many regions or because they *look* as if they are untamed. Ferns are appropriate in moist wild gardens—the species and variety will depend on the particular climate and exposure to sun. Other popular plants include dutchman's breeches, alum root, *Helleborus orientalis*, jack-in-the-pulpit, lily-of-the-valley, lady's slipper, blood root, and trillium for shade. For sunny "meadows" (actual meadows or converted back yards), there are bluets, cardinal flower, *Phlox divaricata*, spring beauty, violets, and cranesbill geranium, as well as such obvious choices as red clover, chicory (bluest of blues), queen anne's lace, black-eyed susans, and—is there anything more appealing?—masses of daisies dancing in the sun.

If space and allergies allow, that noblest of American wildflowers, golden rod, is an ideal choice. Imagine the embarrassment of the early 19th-century writer William Cobett who, having sneered at golden rod, calling it an "accursed stinking thing," was shown a carefully nurtured display of the plant at England's Hampton Court, in full bloom "over the whole length of the edge of the walk, three quarters of a mile long and perhaps thirty feet wide —the most magnificent border, perhaps, in Europe!" All of which reinforces Emerson's well-known definition of a weed as a plant whose virtues have not yet been discovered. (CW)

LOOK FOR:

informal plantings, indigenous plants, maintenance of "natural" settings

Winterthur, near Wilmington, Delaware

It would be difficult to pick any style in any art form that has been popular for as long as topiary. Simply put, topiary is the pruning and training of plants into decorative shapes, and both the word and the practice go back to the ancient world. The word is derived from the Greek *topos*, or place, and the Latin *topiarius*, which Cicero used to mean "the man in charge of the place," or any ornamental gardener. The practice was described as early as 60 A.D. by Pliny the Younger, who wrote about his country garden's boxwood "cut into a thousand different forms."

The Renaissance sparked a renewed interest in all things classical— including topiary. One can trace the route of clipped yew and boxwood from Italy to France to England where, in the reign of Elizabeth I, the gardener and writer William Lawson encouraged readers of his popular book, *The Country Housewife's Garden*, to trim yew into "quaint and playful shapes" such as "swift-running greyhounds."

From England, topiary found its way to colonial America. Here, one of the earliest topiarists was Thomas Hancock, whose garden was the glory of Boston's Beacon Hill in the 1730s. Hancock's letters to his London nurseryman have survived: in 1736 he ordered "100 small yew trees . . . which I'd frame up here to my own fancy." Twenty years later the writer and educator Ezra Stiles praised the Penn family's garden at Springettsburg, near Philadelphia, with its "spruce hedges cut into beautiful figures, etc., all forming the most agreeable variety, and even regular confusion."

Still as popular as ever, topiary is flourishing in the late 20th century as gardeners create "regular confusion" by clipping away at boxwood in the South and at yew, spruce, and ilex in cooler regions. Recently, a new form of topiary has come into its own, thanks to the tireless efforts of artists such as Barbara Gallup, of Stockton, New Jersey. It is called "miniature topiary" and consists of small-leafed vines growing in shaped wire cages to create green and leafy dogs, squirrels, and other small beasts that form ideal table centerpieces and party decorations. (CW)

LOOK FOR:

clipped boxwood, yew, and holly in various shapes

ivy topiary

animal forms

Ladew Topiary Gardens, Harford County, Maryland

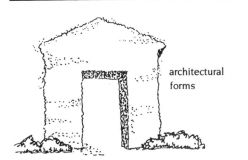

architectural
forms

geometric forms

Who could resist a plant with the name *Nymphea virginalis*? That is the botanical name of our common water lily, the star of water gardens everywhere. Water gardening is an enchanted art form and everything about it is slightly—if beautifully—outrageous. This way of tilling the soil, for instance, hardly requires any tilling. All one needs is a pond (natural or artificial), some plants, and a brace or so of goldfish, properly called *koi*. Koi, by the way, aren't merely decorative: while they certainly are pleasing to the eye, with their gold and silver and black scales glistening in the sun as they dart about among the green plants, they are functional, too. They help the oxygen-carbon dioxide exchange and, by feasting on mosquito larvae, their favorite food, keep those winged pests in line.

The nymphs' names are wonderfully evocative and alluring: they include Sunrise, with a huge yellow flower, Splendida (strawberry red and splendid indeed), Pink Sensation (and it is), White Delight (and *it* is), and Blue Beauty (and . . .).

Lotus speciosum deserves a place beside the virginal nymphs in every pool. These aren't Homer's Egyptian lotuses, but they look just as deliciously enervating with their puffy, pink, cotton-candy blossoms. Other water plants for temperate climates include floating heart (*Nymphoides peltata*), umbrella palm (*Cyperus alternifolius*), and to return to Homer and the Nile, dwarf papyrus (*Cyperus haspans*). (CW)

A Water Garden, Clayton, Missouri

"Taliesen West *is* the desert," said architect Frank Lloyd Wright about his residence outside Scottsdale, Arizona. The startling colors of the desert landscape, particularly as the sun rises and sets, the dramatic juxtaposition of mountain and sky, the arid, sandy ground, and unusual, sun-loving plants provide both a challenge and a constraint for the Southwest gardener. The successful desert garden does not attempt to change nature by introducing lawns, perennial borders, and other conventional horticultural elements. Rather, it adapts cacti and other indigenous plants to the cultivated garden which may at its edges fade indistinguishably in to natural desert landscape. Contrasts of sun and shade, and plants that require minimal attention, contribute to the pleasures of desert gardening. Yucca and aloe, with varieties of cactus and desert carpet wildflowers, provide a satisfactory blend of form and color. Vertical plant materials are often combined with carpet-bedding plants and rocks to reflect the natural appearance of the desert. (DPF)

Desert Garden, Huntington Botanical Gardens, San Marino, California

Legend has it that container gardening began in ancient Greece. Greek women potted fast growing plants in clay pots to surround statues of Adonis. The plants quickly grew, withered, and died in the hot sun, symbolizing the bright, brief life of the mythical lover of Aphrodite. Later, urns became a feature of Italian and Spanish gardens, filled with plants having relatively shallow roots and of unusual shape or color to add interest to terraces or patios.

Container gardens fall into two categories. There is the small private area—a terrace, balcony, or roof-top—where the "ground" is paving material and the gardener must plant in pots, urns, or boxes. And then there is the large paved commercial or public space, sometimes a pedestrian mall or the roof of an underground garage, where flowers and trees are planted in large fixed containers. Examples of the latter are Mellon Square in Pittsburgh, Union Square in San Francisco, and L'Enfant Plaza in Washington, D.C. They may also be seen on roof-top terraces as at the Lever House in New York or Portsmouth Plaza in San Francisco. (DPF)

Constitution Plaza, Hartford, Connecticut

An outgrowth of the 1960s era of social awareness, vest pocket parks have become a feature of many American cities. These small green spaces are oases of relaxation, part of an effort to bring parks to the people. In Manhattan they may provide a place of respite for busy shoppers and office workers; in Miami, a place for the elderly to socialize; in Philadelphia and Baltimore, green gardens for inner city neighborhoods.

These tiny parks are typically the size of a city building lot, or sometimes just left-over spaces between buildings. Where successful, the design expresses the interests of the immediate neighbors. The park may be simply an open, paved area with benches and a shade tree. It may include plantings of yew or juniper for winter interest, generous garden beds for spring bulbs and summer annuals, or plots for growing vegetables. In any case, it is important to use plant material that is durable and adapted to the conditions of their urban settings.

"Neighborhood commons" have been successful in Philadelphia, New York, and Washington when they are understood to be self-help projects—neighbors planting, maintaining, and policing the small areas with a minimum of outside help. Some cities have experimented with a movable version, occupying temporarily vacant spaces until they are used for other purposes. (DPF)

Paley Park, New York City

The pleasures people have derived from contact with plants and beautiful gardens have naturally resulted in their efforts to bring plants indoors to enjoy year round. Potted plants and cut flowers have decorated homes through the ages, but it was not until the London Exposition of 1851 that major plant materials were used in a decorative way indoors. The Crystal Palace, designed and built by Sir Joseph Paxton for this exposition, actually enclosed several existing elm trees. The elms, temperate climate trees, required the periods of cold and dormancy brought about by the change of seasons. The trees could not endure continual warm temperatures and did not survive.

The next advance in interior planting was effected by two factors: the minimal texture, scale, and detail in modern architectural design, and an increased understanding of the requirements of interior plantings. The International Style in architecture, which dominated the 1930s, '40s, and '50s, created steel and glass buildings deliberately devoid of color or ornamentation. Planting offered a logical way to introduce warmth, color, and texture to these sometimes austere buildings. The large expanses of glass admitted the great amount of light essential to plant growth.

The most notable of these early atrium gardens was the lobby of the Ford Foundation in New York City. A wide variety of plants was used, both temperate and tropical; of these, the tropical evergreen plants proved to be the most successful. In the late 1960s, the Hyatt Regency Hotel in Atlanta opened with the first garden atrium of its kind. The concept was so successful that it soon became the hallmark of the Hyatt chain. Later, the John Deere headquarters in Moline, Illinois, was built around a beautiful interior garden which included trees, shrubs, and flowers.

Another development which occurred concurrently with office-building atriums was the development of the enclosed shopping mall with interior planting. In an attempt to make the stores look like small shops lining a city street, "street trees," most often Ficus benjamina, were used in tree grates, along with benches, clocks, and other "street furniture" to complete the illusion. The central atriums or courts of the malls often included large gardens with plant and water displays.

The nursery industry began to develop plants specifically for these interior environments. The greatest concern was light, which is essential to all plant growth. Even the sunniest interior areas admitted only a fraction of the light that the plants were accustomed to in their natural environment. As a result, "acclimatization" procedures were developed to habituate the plants to the low-light situations. Among the more commonly used plants that are able to tolerate low light and consistently warm temperatures are fig tree (Ficus benjamina), dragon tree (Dracaena species), schefflera (Brassaia actinophylla), and kentia palms (Howeia fosteriana). (CM)

Charleston Town Center, Charleston, West Virginia

From 1900 to 1930, garden design was dominated by large estates, but the Great Depression brought an end to this work. What began to emerge in the late 1930s was a reaction against the Beaux Arts tradition of these estates with their formal, symmetrical gardens laid out on axes related to the house. There was, in addition, a reaction to the lifestyle that these estates suggested and an increased interest in the smaller house, designed more with regard to specific site requirements. Because much of the impetus for this new style developed from the traditions in California, it is generally labeled the California School.

The evolving of California gardens showed an increasing emphasis on outdoor living, a life-style adopted, by way of Mexico, from the Moorish tradition of courtyard gardens in Spain. Indeed, the warm and sunny California climate was ideally suited to outdoor living, and the popularity of the home swimming pool added to this trend.

Thomas Church, who studied landscape architecture at the University of California at Berkeley and later at the Harvard Graduate School of Design in the late 1930s, came to embody the new creative spirit of the California School. He practiced in the San Francisco area until his retirement in the late 1970s. The most common features of his gardens were terraces, swimming pools, areas for outdoor play for children, and low-maintenance plant materials such as yew and juniper.

At about this time on the East Coast, a similar development in garden design was occurring at Harvard University. While Walter Gropius was experimenting with new architectural design, a small group of rebellious landscape architects at Harvard's Graduate School of Design, including Garrett Eckbo, James Rose, and Dan Kiley, were similarly searching for a contemporary expression for landscape design. The gardens they created possess a quality totally unlike their Beaux Arts predecessors.

The style of the modern garden can generally be described as

LOOK FOR:

potted flowers

wood trellises

either "asymmetrically geometric," as found in the work of Eckbo and Lawrence Halprin, or "naturalistic," where curving lines predominate. Irregular forms, flowing spaces leading from one to another and relating strongly to both the architecture of the house and the site, were unique contributions of this design. Public landscapes such as parks and plazas follow the same patterns as the private gardens, with fluid geometry, low-maintenance materials such as concrete, brick, and natural wood, and massed evergreen plantings. (CM)

Donnell Garden, Sonoma, California

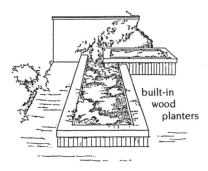

built-in
wood
planters

curving lines

The modern movement attempted to break with the tradition of the Beaux Arts which preceded it and posited a new visual language that was clean, pure, and unadorned. Modern gardens were simple in line and relied heavily on low-maintenance evergreen plants. The trends which followed, now loosely grouped under the rubric, "postmodern," attempt to recapture the sense of history and connection with the visual past that modernism eschewed. Postmodernism is perhaps best described as an attitude which places a high value on context, a sense of history, the importance of color, and preference for complexity and ambiguity over the "clarity" of the modernists.

While modern gardens were developing, traditional or classical gardens continued to be constructed. Thus the abrupt break with the past that architecture experienced did not occur as strongly in landscape architecture where both traditional and modern gardens continued to be produced, sometimes by the same designer. The present re-emergence of historical and classical forms in postmodern garden design is actually a continuation of a practice that was never totally lost.

Postmodern gardens are only beginning to emerge, but important elements so far include a variety of sculptural pieces, such as benches, urns, columns, and trellises. The supply of these items is beginning to meet the demand, and contemporary designers, for the first time, have access to a wide array of such items to choose from. The use of grids for pattern or as an organizing element in postmodern design has brought about a renewed interest in the use of lattice. In addition, color has finally found its way back into gardens, largely in the form of annuals and perennials.

In public gardens, however, modern design became almost exclusively the vocabulary of the '40s, '50s and '60s. Unfortunately these originally inventive designs, such as Lawrence Halprin's Lovejoy Fountain (now the Ira Keller Fountain) in Portland, Oregon, were often imitated and lost much of their original visual excitement. The postmodern plazas and courtyards that are being designed and built today differ from these modern designs in several major ways. There is less regularity in the overall design, more unexpected twists and turns in the plan, more colorful patterning, and more collaboration with artists as an integral part of the plan. An important example of these trends is August Perez and Associates' Piazza d'Italia in New Orleans, a lively combination of color, neon, and sculpture with a fanciful fountain by Charles Moore, and Gas Works Park in Seattle by Richard Haag, a reclamation of an industrial site and its relics for contemporary recreation.

Another outstanding example of the new thrust in the design of public plazas comes from the SWA Group, landscape architects in California who designed Harlequin Plaza in Denver, Colorado. The plaza itself is surrounded by mirrored office buildings but gives a dramatic view out to the Rocky Mountains. Located over a parking garage and pierced by numerous pieces of mechanical equipment, the plaza was a difficult site. The SWA Group encased these odd elements in mirrored glass as well, creating an exchange of reflections and space. The floor is a large-scale, black-and-white checkerboard, and the walls are red and purple. It is at once a stage set where performances are given, a garden courtyard for lunchtime use, and, through its geometry, a visual link with the mountains beyond. The end result is a corporate courtyard with a colorful and whimsical appearance characteristic of the Postmodern approach to design. (CM)

Harlequin Plaza, Denver, Colorado

Balmori, D., D. McGuire, and E. McPeck. *Beatrix Farrand's American Landscapes.* New York: Sagapress, 1985.

Dutton, Joan P. *Enjoying America: Gardens.* New York: Reynal & Co., 1958.

Fitch, J. M. and F. F. Rockwell. *Treasury of American Gardens.* New York: Harper Bros., Chanticleer Press, 1956.

Jellico, Geoffrey Alan. *The Landscape of Man.* New York: Viking Press, 1975.

Leighton, Anne. *American Gardens in the Eighteenth Century: "For Use or for Delight."* Boston: Houghton Mifflin, 1976.

Maccubbin, Robert, and Peter Martin. *British and American Gardening in the Eighteenth Century.* Williamsburg, Virginia: Colonial Williamsburg Foundation, 1984.

McGourty, Frederick (ed.). *American Gardens: A Traveler's Guide.* New York: Brooklyn Botanic Garden, 1970

Newton, Norman. *Design on the Land.* Cambridge: Harvard University Press, Belknap Press, 1971.

Ray, M. H., and R. P. Nicholls. *A Guide to Significant and Historic Gardens of America.* Athens, Georgia: Agee Publishers, 1983.

Samuels, Ellen R., "Bulletin of American Garden History" (periodical), Box 397A, Planetarium Station, New York, 10024.

Simonds, John Ormsbee. *Earthscape: A Manual of Environmental Planning.* New York: McGraw-Hill, 1978.

Thacker, Christopher. *The History of Gardens.* Berkeley: University of California Press, 1979.

SELECTED ADDITIONAL RESOURCES

American Horticultural Society, 7931 E. Boulevard Dr., Alexandria, VA 22308

American Society of Landscape Architects, 1733 Connecticut Ave. N.W., Washington, DC 20009

Arnold Arboretum, The Arborway, Jamaica Plain, MA 02130

Brooklyn Botanic Garden, 1000 Washington Ave., Brooklyn, NY 11225

Callaway Gardens, Pine Mountain, GA 31822

Chicago Botanic Garden, Lake Cook Road, Glencoe, IL 60022

Denver Botanic Gardens, 900 York St., Denver, CO 80206

Garden Club of America, 598 Madison Ave., New York, NY 10022

Garfield Park Conservatory, 300 N. Central Park Ave., Chicago, IL 60624

Longwood Gardens, Kennett Square, PA 19348

Los Angeles State and County Arboretum, N. Baldwin Ave., Los Angeles, CA 90031

Massachusetts Horticultural Society, 300 Massachusetts Ave., Boston, MA 02115

Missouri Botanical Garden, 2315 Tower Grove Ave., St. Louis, MO 63110

Morris Arboretum, 9414 Meadowbrook Lane, Philadelphia, PA 19118

National Arboretum, 3501 New York Ave., N.W., Washington, DC 20002

New York Botanical Garden, Bronx Park, NY 10458

Pennsylvania Horticultural Society, 425 Walnut Street, Philadelphia, PA 19106

Perennial Plant Association, Box 86, Kensington, CT 06037

Philadelphia Flower Show, Civic Center, Philadelphia, PA (March)

Rancho Santa Ana Botanic Garden, 1500 N. College Ave., Claremont, CA 91711

Golden Gate State Park, Fulton Street, San Francisco, CA 94121

University of Washington Arboretum, Madison and 31st Street, Seattle, WA 98105

GARDENS IN THE TEXT OPEN TO THE PUBLIC

California:	Golden Gate Park, San Francisco, 29
	La Cuesta Encantada, San Simeon, 10
	Palace of Fine Arts, San Francisco, 35
	Portsmouth Plaza, San Francisco, 54
	Union Square, San Francisco, 54
	Huntington Botanical Gardens, 53
Colorado:	Harlequin Plaza, Denver, 61
Connecticut:	Constitution Plaza, Hartford, 54
	White Flower Farm, Litchfield, 39
Delaware:	Winterthur, near Wilmington, 48, 49
District of Columbia:	Dumbarton Oaks, 24, 25, 37
	L'Enfant Plaza, 54
	Tudor Place, 19
Florida:	Gonzalez-Alvarez House, St. Augustine, 10, 11